EXTREME SCIENCE EXPLORERS

EXPLORE THE MILKY WAY

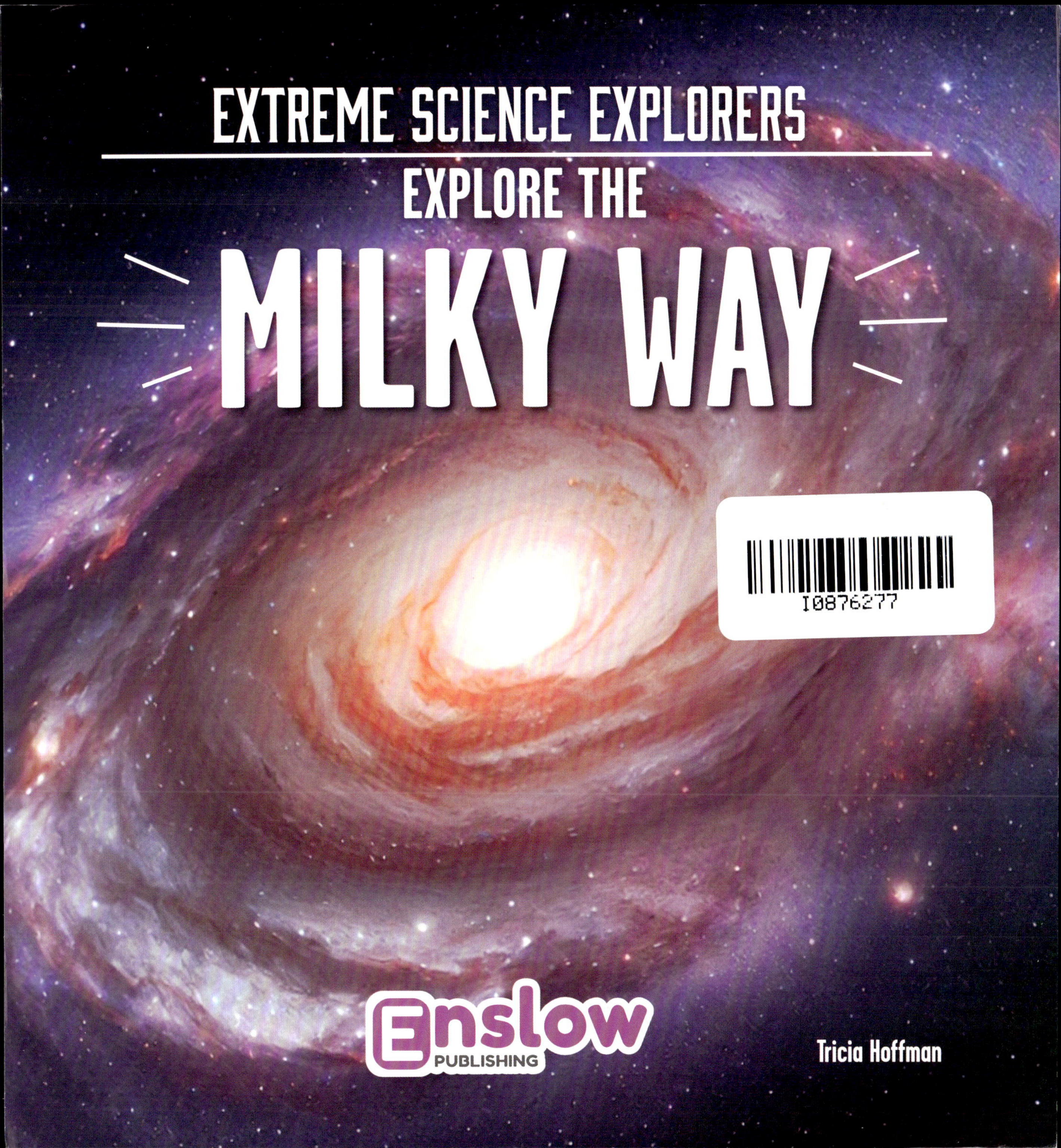

Enslow PUBLISHING

Tricia Hoffman

Please visit our website, www.enslow.com. For a free color catalog of all our high-quality books, call toll free 1-800-398-2504 or fax 1-877-980-4454

Published in 2027 by
Enslow Publishing
2544 Clinton Street
Buffalo, NY 14224

Portions of this work were originally authored by Heather Moore Niver and published as *Fantastic Science Journeys: A Trip Through the Milky Way.* All new material in this edition is authored by Tricia Hoffman.

Cataloging-in-Publication Data
Names: Hoffman, Tricia.
Title: Explore the Milky Way / Tricia Hoffman.
Description: Buffalo, NY : Enslow Publishing, 2027. | Series: Extreme science explorers | Includes glossary and index.
Identifiers: ISBN 9781978549081 (pbk.) | ISBN 9781978549098 (library bound) | ISBN 9781978549104 (ebook)
Subjects: LCSH: Milky Way--Juvenile literature. | Galaxies--Juvenile literature.
Classification: LCC QB857.7 H644 2027 | DDC 523.113--dc23

Printed in China

Photos Credits: Cover, p. 1 nednapa/Shutterstock.com; p. 3 ANON MUENPROM/Shutterstock.com; p. 4 Photobond/Shutterstock.com; p. 7 NASA/NASA; p. 8 Diego Barucco/Shutterstock.com; p. 8 Savvapanf Photo/Shutterstock.com; p. 9 Katrine Butushina/Shutterstock.com; p. 10 Nik Coli/Shutterstock.com; p. 12 Wikipedia/Wikipedia; p. 13 VectorMine/Shutterstock.com; p. 15 NASA/NASA; p. 16 Wikipedia/Wikipedia; p. 19 Milky Way Galactic Centre/Shutterstock.com; p. 20 NASA, ESA, CSA, Ralf Crawford (STScI)/NASA; p. 23 NASA/NASA.com; p. 26 remotevfx.com/Shutterstock.com; p. 28 Noah Zastrow/Shutterstock.com; p. 31 Sergiy Nigeruk/Shutterstock.com; p. 14, 17 Wikipedia/Wikipedia; p. 6, 24 muratart/Shutterstock.com

CPSIA compliance information: Batch #QSENS27: For further information, contact Enslow Publishing, New York, New York, at 1-800-398-2504.

TABLE OF CONTENTS

EXPLORING OUTER SPACE

Have you ever stared up at the sky on a dark night? The night sky is home to **planets** and moons and beautiful sparkling stars. During the day we can see the sun, and sometimes the moon and other planets too. There's so much out there. Far more than what the eye can see!

The sky is a vast and wondrous place. Some humans have gone into space, but not many people get that opportunity. Let's imagine we can fly to outer space and explore wherever we want. We could explore far across our **galaxy**. Let's go!

THAT'S EXTREME!

*The Milky Way and other galaxies can be seen from Earth. Just south of the **equator**, you can see two dwarf galaxies called the Large Magellanic Cloud and the Small Magellanic Cloud. They're named after the explorer Ferdinand Magellan.*

The biggest galaxies hardly have any gas or dust. They can have more than one trillion stars, though! Almost all stars belong to galaxies.

Earth is about halfway between the edge and the center of the Milky Way.

THE MILKY WAY

We live in a galaxy called the Milky Way. A galaxy is made up of stars, gases, and dust that move through the **universe** together. The Milky Way is called a barred spiral galaxy, named for its whirling arms and the bar shape across the middle of it. When we see a wide band of light, we know that's the center of the Milky Way!

The Milky Way is one of billions of galaxies in our universe. The sun and its planets, including Earth, are all part of the Milky Way. It contains more than 200 billion stars, along with dust and gas.

THAT'S EXTREME!

In the 1920s, astronomer Edwin Hubble realized there was more than one galaxy in space. Before then, scientists had thought all the stars were part of the Milky Way. He also figured out that the universe was constantly getting bigger.

OUR SOLAR SYSTEM

There are eight planets in our **solar system**: Mercury, Venus, Earth, Mars, Jupiter, Saturn, Uranus, and Neptune. Mercury and Venus are between Earth and the sun. Neptune, the eighth planet, is the furthest away from the sun. It's about 2.8 billion miles (4.5 billion km) away!

There's a band of big rocks between Mars and Jupiter called an asteroid belt. It sits between the rocky planets that are closer to the sun and the outer planets that are mostly made of gas. Far past Neptune is another big area called the Kuiper (KY-puhr) Belt. It is full of icy objects, including dwarf planets like Pluto.

THAT'S EXTREME!

There are five dwarf planets in our galaxy: Ceres, Makemake, Haumea, Eris, and Pluto.

Along with the planets and dwarf planets, our solar system also has moons, comets, and other bodies that all circle the sun.

The Andromeda Galaxy is 2.5 million ***light-years*** away, but you can see it from Earth, sometimes even without binoculars!

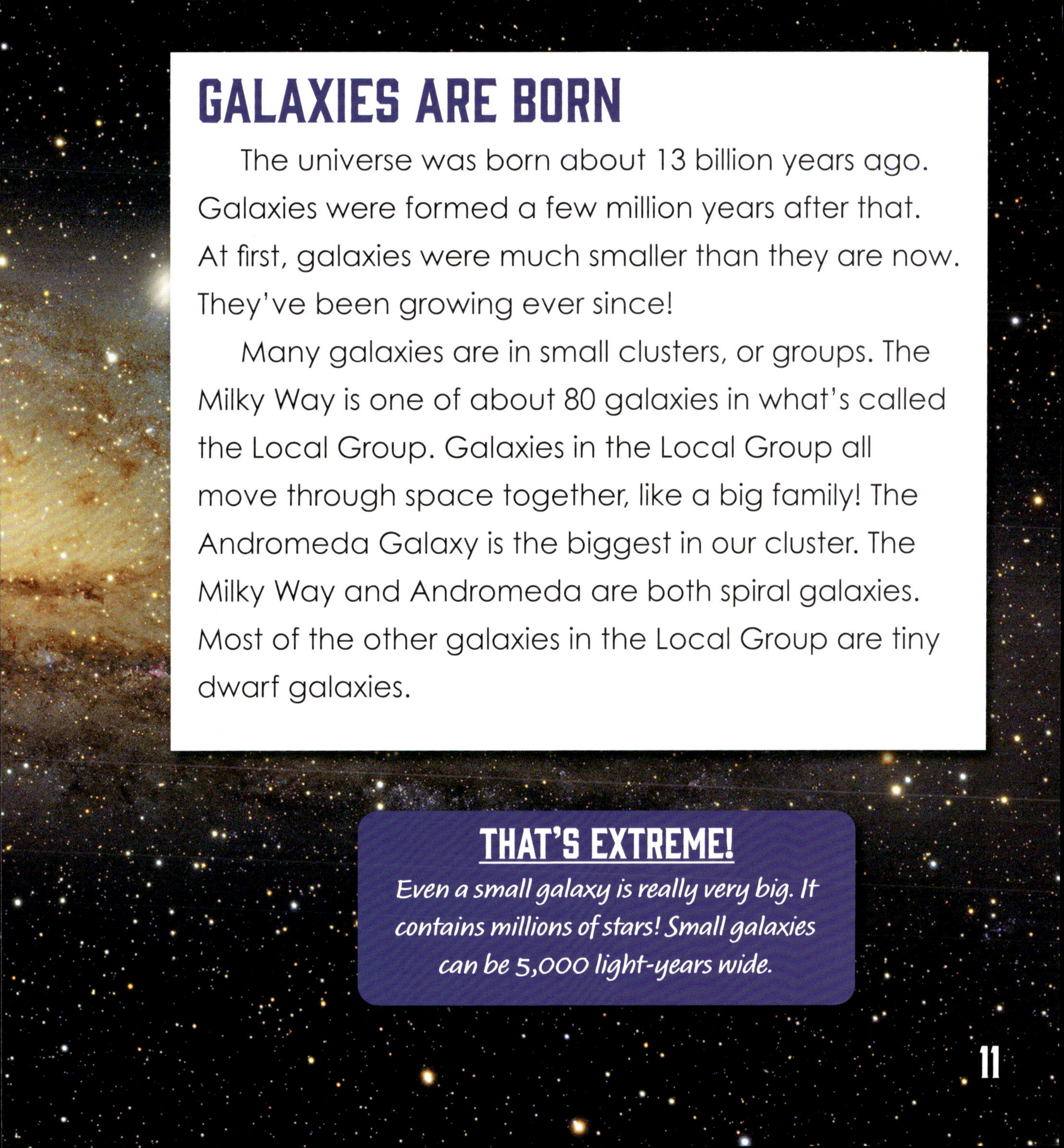

GALAXIES ARE BORN

The universe was born about 13 billion years ago. Galaxies were formed a few million years after that. At first, galaxies were much smaller than they are now. They've been growing ever since!

Many galaxies are in small clusters, or groups. The Milky Way is one of about 80 galaxies in what's called the Local Group. Galaxies in the Local Group all move through space together, like a big family! The Andromeda Galaxy is the biggest in our cluster. The Milky Way and Andromeda are both spiral galaxies. Most of the other galaxies in the Local Group are tiny dwarf galaxies.

THAT'S EXTREME!

Even a small galaxy is really very big. It contains millions of stars! Small galaxies can be 5,000 light-years wide.

ALL SHAPES AND SIZES

Beyond the Milky Way are galaxies of all shapes and sizes. **Elliptical** galaxies are the largest. They are oval or shaped like a football. **Irregular** galaxies are uncommon and don't really have a set shape.

Spiral galaxies such as the Milky Way are shaped like pinwheels. Older stars are near the center. New stars are created from the dust and gas found in the pinwheel's arms. Light can pass through the Milky Way from one side to the other, but it takes 100,000 years because the galaxy is so big. That means the Milky Way is 100,000 light-years across!

THAT'S EXTREME!

The Milky Way is just one of billions of spiral galaxies in the universe.

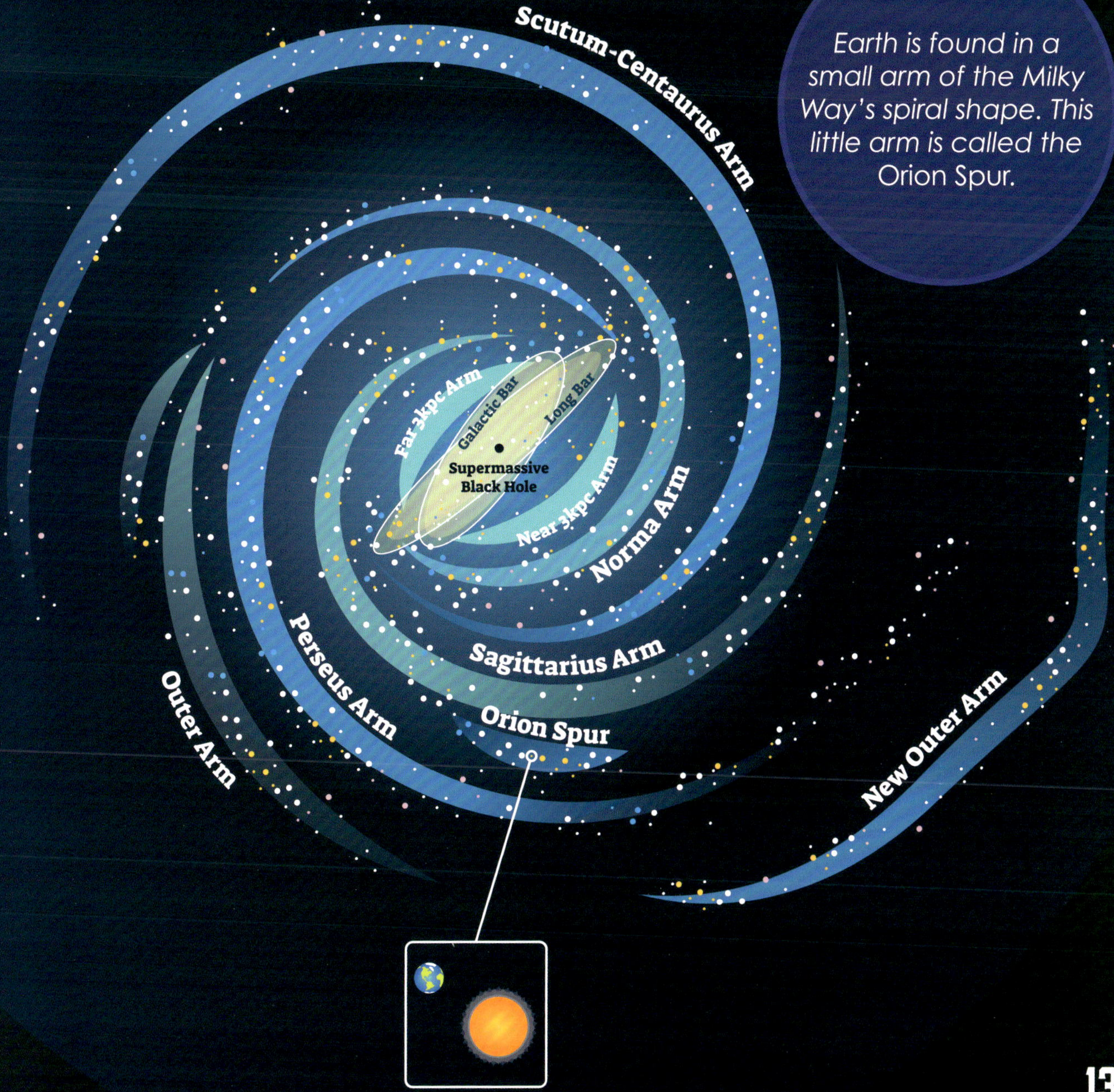

Earth is found in a small arm of the Milky Way's spiral shape. This little arm is called the Orion Spur.

MAPPING THE MILKY WAY

It's not easy to map out the Milky Way because it's so large. The Milky Way has two to four spiral arms that start at a central bar. The Milky Way also has smaller bars and spurs, or branches.

Scientists think the arms are created by waves that move through the galaxy, causing gas and dust to clump together in places. And in the middle of all this is one of the biggest mysteries yet: a **black hole**. A black hole is an area of space where **gravity** is so strong that nothing can escape from it!

THAT'S EXTREME!

There are different types of black holes. Stellar black holes form from dying stars. Supermassive black holes are found in the middle of galaxies.

Stellar black hole (left) in the spiral galaxy NGC 300.

Black holes get their name because they're invisible. Even light can't escape from them.

THE GALACTIC BULGE

The Milky Way's arms make a flat disk. At the center is what's called a "galactic bulge." It's stuffed so full of stars, gas, and dust that it blocks our view of stars in it and on the other side of the Milky Way.

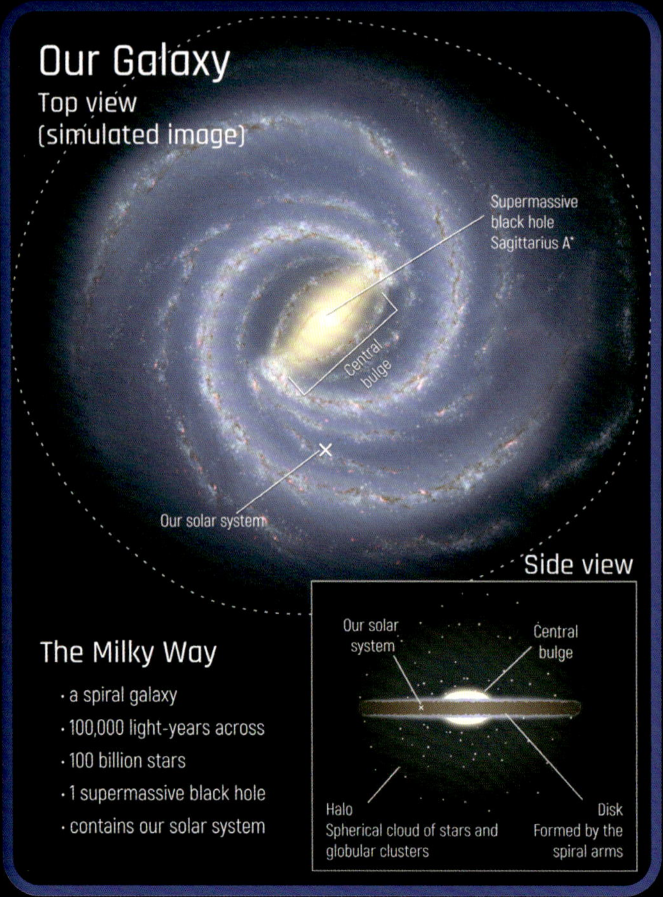

A galactic bulge is usually found in spiral galaxies. It is the dense area of stars at the center.

THAT'S EXTREME!

Above and below the disk are two giant bubbles. The bubbles each have a ***jet*** *of matter that's 27,000 light-years long!*

The bulge and arms are the most eye-catching parts of the Milky Way, but it also has a round **halo** made of hot gas, old stars, and **globular clusters**. This halo is so big that it stretches for hundreds of thousands of light-years from the center! Scientists think the halo has two parts, an inner halo and an outer halo. The stars in these two halos formed in different ways.

SUPERMASSIVE BLACK HOLE

Studying outer space can be challenging. Scientists have an even bigger challenge when studying what's at the very center of the Milky Way. That's because lots of dust clouds and gas make it hard to see exactly what's there.

At the center of the Milky Way is a supermassive black hole. Black holes have very strong gravity. They can be studied by looking at how things react to the pull of gravity when they get close to the black hole. Black holes can spin, and their spin changes how things move around them. When a black hole spins faster, it affects the motion of nearby matter even more.

THAT'S EXTREME!

In 2014, scientists discovered a galaxy that has not one but three supermassive black holes at its center!

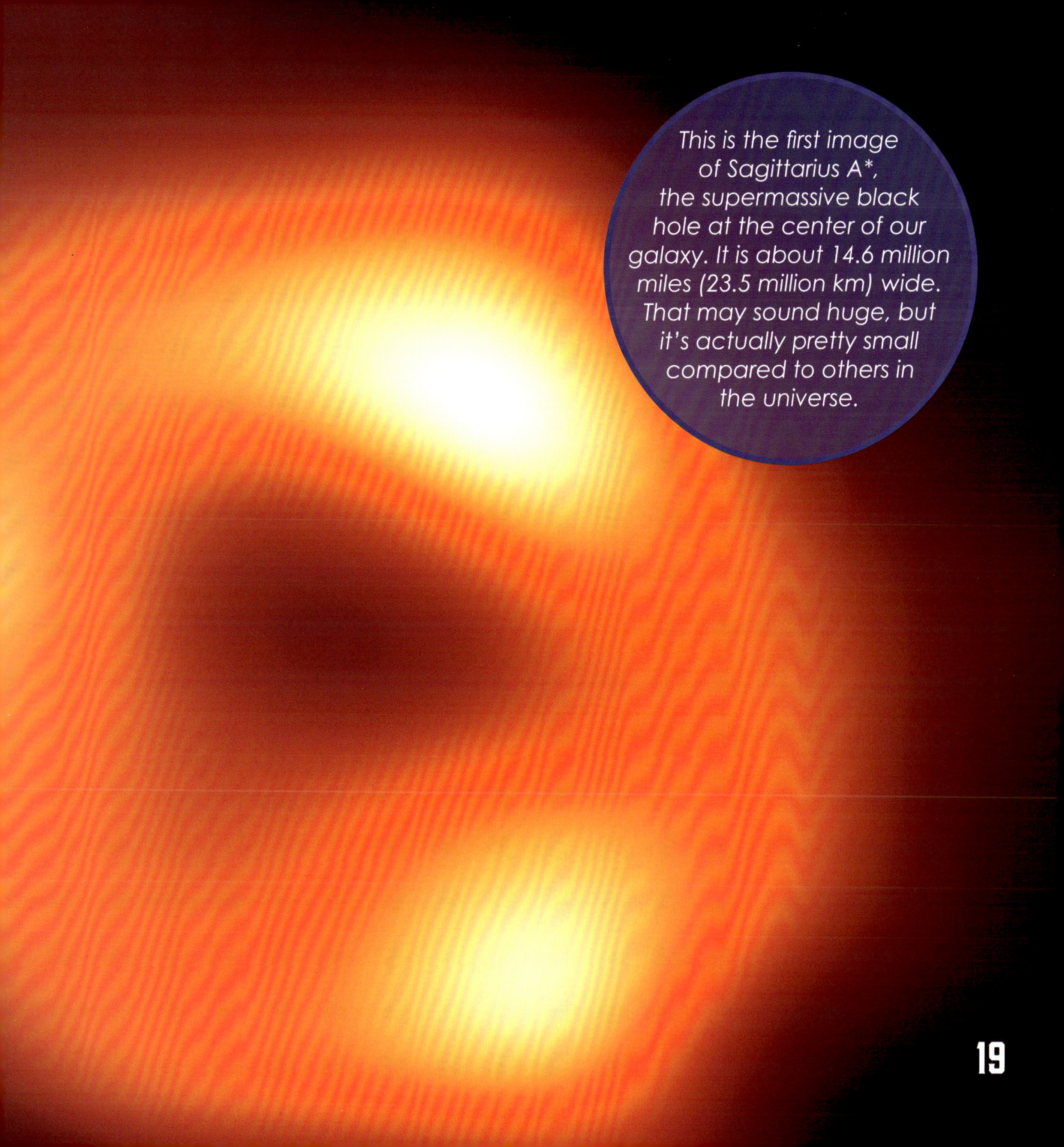

This is the first image of Sagittarius A, the supermassive black hole at the center of our galaxy. It is about 14.6 million miles (23.5 million km) wide. That may sound huge, but it's actually pretty small compared to others in the universe.*

BIGGER AND BIGGER

The Milky Way's black hole was not always as big as it is now. It started out much smaller. Thanks to gravity, it keeps pulling in more objects and getting bigger. Scientists think this black hole gobbles up anything that gets close to it. It might snack on dust, gas, stars, and even asteroids!

THAT'S EXTREME!

Some astronomers call the black hole a monster because it eats up so much stuff! They think it's very destructive. But they don't live forever! They disappear over time.

Sometimes bright flares, or flashes of light, surround the black hole. These light shows can last up to an hour! The light show near the black hole comes from gas clouds being trapped inside.

Sagittarius A is surrounded by a swirling disk of hot gas. The black hole's gravity bends light from the far side of the disk, making it look like it's wrapping around the black hole.*

INVISIBLE DARK MATTER

The Milky Way is chock full of dust, gas, and stars. But there's even more to our galaxy than that. It's also made up of dark matter.

Unfortunately, we can't see dark matter, even from outer space. That's because it's invisible. Because of this, scientists aren't sure what it's made of! We can't see dark matter because it doesn't interact with light. It doesn't **emit**, **absorb**, or reflect it.

Scientists learn about dark matter by studying the objects around it, like they do with black holes. People are still trying to understand dark matter and what it does to the Milky Way.

THAT'S EXTREME!

Dark matter makes up about 90 percent of the Milky Way.

Dark matter is one of the biggest mysteries of space. This image from the Hubble Space Telescope shows a ghostly "ring" of dark matter in a galaxy cluster.

Scientists say Andromeda has smashed into other galaxies in the past.

CRASHING IN SPACE

Space may seem like a wide open area, but galaxies smash into each other sometimes! That goes for the Milky Way too.

The Milky Way will run into the Andromeda Galaxy in about 4 billion years. These two galaxies are speeding toward each other at about 70 miles (112 km) per second! When this happens, it will change the shape of both galaxies.

But what else happens when galaxies crash into each other? They both undergo big changes. Gas and dust get pushed together, which helps form new stars. The galaxies are likely to change shape. Eventually the two galaxies will combine to form a single, larger galaxy.

THAT'S EXTREME!

When galaxies collide, changes don't happen instantly. It takes millions or billions of years!

RED DWARFS

Most of the stars in the Milky Way are called red dwarfs. These tiny stars are smaller than the sun—about one-tenth its size. Red dwarfs are also cooler than the sun and less bright.

There are about 4.5 billion red dwarfs in the Milky Way. The red dwarf that's closest to Earth is about 12 light-years away. Scientists think there could be other life living near these stars on planets much like Earth! Red dwarf stars live for about 2.5 trillion years, which is much longer than larger stars.

THAT'S EXTREME!

Three out of every four stars in the Milky Way are red dwarf stars. But they are often too dim to see from Earth.

The sun is a yellow dwarf star. Red dwarf stars live longer than our sun will last.

The next time you look at the night sky, think about all there is to the universe—and how much more there still is to discover.

A UNIVERSE OF INFORMATION

Scientists still have plenty to learn about our galaxy and our universe. New planets and stars are still being discovered. Scientists are always hard at work on new ways to measure and figure out the exact shape of it. No one knows exactly what might be discovered!

Our galaxy rotates, or spins around, about once every 200 million years. More than 200 billion stars call the Milky Way home. And there's enough matter in this galaxy to make billions more stars! The Milky Way is an amazing place.

THAT'S EXTREME!

The name "Milky Way" comes from the ancient Greeks. They thought the galaxy looked like milk that was spilled across the sky.

GLOSSARY

absorb: to soak up something

black hole: a huge amount of matter packed in a tiny space, with such strong gravity nothing can get out

elliptical: having an oval or football shape

emit: to produce or send out something

equator: the imaginary line that circles the middle of Earth

galaxy: a large group of stars, planets, gas, and dust that form a unit within the universe

globular cluster: a ball-shaped group of stars

gravity: a force that pulls objects toward the center of a planet or star

halo: a circle of light that shines around a planet or galaxy

irregular: not even or balanced

jet: a powerful rush of matter through a narrow space

light-year: the distance light can travel in one year

planet: a large object in space that circles a star

solar system: the sun and all the space objects that orbit it, including the planets and their moons

universe: all existing matter and space

MORE INFORMATION

BOOKS

Bauer, Marion Dane. *The Milky Way*. New York, NY: Simon Spotlight, 2025.

Gater, Will. *The Mysteries of the Universe*. London, UK: DK Children, 2020.

Hicks, John. *Awesome Space Facts for Kids*. Fargo, ND: Spotlight Media, 2024.

WEBSITES

Milky Way Galaxy

https://kids.nationalgeographic.com/space/article/milky-way

Read more about the Milky Way and watch some videos that are out of this world!

Space Facts: Galaxy Facts for Kids

sciencekids.co.nz/sciencefacts/space/galaxies.html

Rocket on over to this site for more fun galaxy facts and information!

INDEX